To Miranda

Magical Insights & Inspirations
by
John Awen & Jhyenan O'Shea

May this book give you
inspiration, Clarity +
strength.

Much love on
your journey.
John Awen

Magical Insights & Inspirations
ISBN 978-1-907963-18-6

Published by
Hedge Witchery Books
www.hedge-witcherybooks.com

We are also very honoured to have as guest writers, Fiona Magpie Witch, Laura Bos. What wonderful, inspirational and beautiful words they have given us for this book. Our Love and Thanks goes out to them along with our heartfelt Blessings of Love and Light...)0(...

The Lady calls, I hear her sweet Voice

As my soul arises to her Tune

Deep within me, my heart Sings

As I celebrate my Life

The wonder of Friends

The joy of Family

The gift of Love Eternal

The beauty of Her Earth

The divine night Sky

Her full, radiant beautiful Moon

She is within, without and all Around

As I feel her pulse of life surge through Me

I dance to her beat, I sway to her Rhythm

Thank you, O Sacred Goddess who Shines Above for the sacred gifts of Life and Love

Blessed Be

)O(

An Invocation

I Call Upon the Darkness Bright

Lead Me from Day and Through the Night

Silvery Lady, of the Night Above

Encompass and Surround Me with Your Love

Horned Hunter of the Night

Lead Me through the Darkness Bright

Encompass and Surround Me with your Love

From the Earth Below to the Sky up Above

Elements! Of Land and Sea

Surround and Encompass Me

Hear My Call, Air and Fire!

At My Side, By My Desire!

Here in My Perfect Circle Cast

I Find thy Peace from Future to Past

Here in this Perfect Sacred Space

Between Worlds Is My Special Place

In Thy Presence, I Honour Thee

In Perfect Love and Harmony

Blessed Be

)O(

The Lady

O Great Goddess of the Tides and Seas

Who cleanses the souls of you and Me

By Her ebb and flow the rivers Run

From the sand laden shore off into the Sun

The Lady's beauty is for all to See

She flows within the hearts of you and Me

She brings us love and joy and Harmony

As Her Stars shine brightly in the skies Above

And Her moon glows with Her light and Love

I stand between worlds, below and Above

In this sacred circle, I Invoke Her Name

Come Join me, my Lady, as I light Her Flame

As time stands still, all around Me

The Lady descends, in her radiant Beauty

Truly blessed am I this Day

As the Lady comes my Way

She live within me, within us All

Hear her Voice, Heed her Call

Her Love flows as the tides and the Seas

As we walk our path with Blessed Be's

)O(

Maiden, Mother, Crone

As the Maiden, our Lady she laughs and Sings

To many hearts, great joy she Brings

She is full of life, and sings and Dances

Twirls and jumps and lightly Prances

Carefree, her beauty flows and Spills

Upon the earth, our souls it Fills

Silver stars shimmer and Shine

To show the way to the Divine

From Maiden to Mother she Becomes

As the flower blossoms from bud to Bloom

Beautiful as a silver rose is She

As she weaves her web for you and Me

As the Mother, she brings us Stability

And the love and protection of Family

She is with child, glowing and Free

Her beauty shines down for all to See

As the wheel turns Her wisdoms Grown

From the loving Mother to the loving Crone

She nurtures, protects and watches over Us

Her love abounds in perfect trust

So Mote it Be

In Her Perfect Love and Harmony

)0(

Beltane Awakening

O Great Mother Goddess, as you rise from your Sleep

Hear our calls unto thee from the winters Deep

Now you are stirring and to us you Return

Rested and refreshed as the wheel again Turns

The Lord is waiting with a patient Hand

As your bring new life upon the Land

Together again ye both shall Be

In perfect love and Harmony

As the maiden you Appear

At this time of the Year

With your beauty and Grace

May you Bless us your Children

As we Honour you in this our Sacred Space

Blessed Be)O(

Call of Power

I Call on the Lady......Bold and Bright

Hear My Call on this Darkest Night

I Invoke the Elements By My Desire

Come Now. Water, Earth, Air and Fire!

Send Me Your Strength, Power and Might

As I Walk Through the Darkness into the Light

Mystical, Magickal Dragons of the Night

Come Now, Attend Me in Your Roaring Flight

Send Forth Your Protection as You Fly Around

Encompass Me, Surround Me, Your Power Abounds

Between Realms and Worlds I Safely Stand

Great Father, Lord, I Take Thy Hand

My Circle is Cast, Strong and True

I am Safe Here...Because of You

In Thy Sacred Love and Harmony

In Thy Perfect Light.....So Mote it Be!

)O(

The Ancient Mother Goddess

Ancient Mother of the Moon and the Seas

Hear my call as I come before Thee

In the ancient swirling mists of Time

I hear thy song, I hear thy Rhyme

The pulse of the earth beats with a vibrant Hum

The night is over, the day is Begun

I stand in awe, at the beauty of it All

Great Mother Goddess, Take my hand, May I not stumble, May I not

Fall

As we walk through this new day

May we walk in thy light, the Blessed Way

May thy light be both within and Without

May it surround and encircle me around and About

Great Mother of all that I See

May you forever walk beside Me

Give me the wisdom and grace to accept the good with the Bad

Laugh with me when I am Happy, Comfort Me when I'm Sad

May I forever sing your Blessed Song

Throughout the Day and Night Long

When Thy beautiful, glowing moon, rises and Shines

Blessed am I, Thy Daughter, for I am Thyne

In Perfect Love and Harmony

In Love and Light

So Mote it Be!

)O(

Prayer to the Lady

Gracious Goddess

Who art Maiden, Mother, Crone

Celebrated be your Blessed Name

Help me to live in Peace upon your Earth

Grant me safety within your Arms

Guide me along my chosen Path

And show me your eternal Love

Lead me safely to the cauldron of Rebirth

For it is your Spirit that lives within Me

It surrounds and Protects Me

For Ever Eternal

So Mote it Be

)O(

Picture by Laura Bos

A Healing Prayer

Sacred Mother and Father of All

Hear me as to Thee I Call

Send forth thy Healing Energies

Upon all those in great Need

Wrap them in your Warm Embrace

Heal and Hold them within your Grace

Elements, Guardians of Old!

Send forth your Healing Powers Bold

Earth, Air, Water and Fire

Hear my Call, By my Desire

Your Healing Light, Please Bestow

Your Children are in need of your Loving Glow

Hear my Prayer as I call to Thee

As I do will... So Mote it Be

A Prayer to the Father

Father, Hear Me as I grow and learn

Cernunnos, Osiris and Mighty Herne

Lord of the Mountains, the Wood and Tree

Keeper of Places Wild and Free

Across the Land thy Spirit Roams

Great Hunter, Protector of our Home

My Father, My Lover, the Ancient One

Who brings the Dawn and the Rising Sun

I give thanks to thee for all that you've done

Lead and guide me through all of my life

Keep me from harm and trouble and strife

I honor thee in the ancient ways

Bless all of my nights and all of my days

As I come before you on bended knee

O Mighty Father, Hear me as I call to thee

)O(

Father

Father God of all the Wild

I am Thy Daughter, I am Thy Child

Lord of the Forest, Mountain and Tree

Hear me as I call to Thee

Lord Cernunnos, Herne of the Night

Attend my circle, by the moonlight's Bright

Bring the balance of your male Energies

The light and the dark in their Harmonies

Bring your might, power, strength and Mirth

Upon the realm of Her Mother's Earth

The Lord and Lady hand in Hand

Together they rule throughout the Land

As the Wheel turns, the day has Begun

Goddess of the Moon, Lord of the Sun

Within Me, Without, Above and Below

May your guiding light forever Glow

In Perfect Trust and Harmony

In Love and Light… So Mote it Be!

Painting by Laura Bos

An Invocation

Ancient Mother of the Moonlight Bright

Who Lights the way in the darkest Night

Triple Goddess, Maiden, Mother and Crone

Ancient Father of the Forest, Rock and Stone

Green man of the wild Glade

Horned Hunter of the Sharpest Blade

Hear my call...Hear my Plea

Hear me as I come to Thee

Lend me your wisdom, beauty and Grace

Descend to my Circle, my sacred Space

Lend me your power, your strength and Might

Lead me from darkness and into the Light

Give me courage as I walk upon my Path

May I always find Thy home and Hearth

Great Mother of Nature and all that I See

Hear my words as I come to Thee

Great Father of Stone, Mountain and Tree

Hear my words as I come to Thee

May I walk in Thy blessed Love and Light

Guide my feet both day and Night

In Thy Perfect Love and Harmony

With all that I am… So Mote it Be!

)O(

The God and Goddess

Mother Goddess of the dusky night and Autumn's Fall

Who touches us with her radiant beauty one and All

Father of the Mountains, Forest and Sacred Tree

I ask that you hear us as we call to Thee

I give reverence to you both, Lord and Lady Bright

I Revel in your union of Love and Light

Great Goddess of the ocean's Flow

Of the moon above in her luminous Glow

Great God of the Wild who roams Her Earth Free

Known by many names may you Be

I bow before you in this sacred Space

To Nature we come in thy beauty and Grace

As we join with the Elements and thy pure Energies

As the children of thy Earth, we are blessed and Free

We breathe in your power, the breath of Life

We dispel the stress of our everyday Life

In thy perfect love and Harmony

As we do will... So Mote it Be!

The Elements

Earth

Direction: North, Colour: Green.

Firmly beneath my Feet, I feel the solid Earth

Rich and moist, the place of my Birth

It exists in it dependable solid Stability

Noble Element! Ground and Centre Me

It holds secrets buried deep Within

It enwraps and enfolds me, its magick Begins

It births crystals, stone, rock and Tree

It brings forth its hue of green Energies

It removes all self-doubt and Negativity

It brings forth the rose, the flower the Tree

It holds and sustains life in its purest Beauty

It cradles the oceans that break on the Shore

It is the strength of the mountains for Evermore

It is my foundation, my home, my sacred Space

May I remain centered and grounded in my special Place

In Perfect Love and Harmony

I honour thee upon bended Knee

In Love and Light

So Mote it Be!

Air

Direction: East, Colour: Yellow

O Great Element of Air, of the winds and the Breeze

Ye that carries the birds and rustles the Trees

Bringer of the mighty winds, from the East ye Hail

Where the sailor waits and sets his Sail

I bow before you as I honour Thee

Lend me your strength, power and Prosperity

Ye that fans the Blessed Fire

Work my will… By my Desire!

Upon my path this very Day

Aid me walking the Blessed Way

May your winds blow and caress Me

Remove from my life all Negativity

So Mote it Be!

Fire

Direction: East, Colour: Orange

O Great Element of Fire! That cleanses and Purifies

Ye that flickers and dances from Earth to Sky

Ye brings warmth and security within thy sacred Flame

From the South ye hail as I call thy Name

Passion and Strength are born of Thee

The flame of life burns deep within Me

By candle, and hearth and blessed Bonfire

Work my will, by my Desire!

May you light my path this very Day

As I walk my life the Blessed Way

I bow before you as I honour Thee

Lend me your strength, passion and Vitality

That I may share with those I Know

May your flame burn and forever Grow

So Mote it Be!

Water

Direction: West, Colour: Blue

O Great Element of Water... As You flow through Me

You wash and cleanse the inner Me

You purify, you soothe, you calm Me

You embrace me in your pure Beauty

You flow as a tide, breaking on the distant Shore

You bring positive emotions, You remove all Flaws

You are crystal clear, in the sparkling depths Below

You are Her Blood, Her Life's force Glow

You are all around, within, above and Below

You, in your Power, wear away and Erode

You are found in places no one else Goes

You are a noble quarter, majestic and Fluid

You come to circle, be it for witch or Druid

I embrace your life giving Energies

In Perfect Trust and Harmony... So Mote it Be!

)O(

Akasha

O Great Spirit, Akasha. Ancient of Old

That binds the Elements Fourfold

You entwine them all with your majestic Might

May you join my Circle, May you attend my Rite

Spirit of all that lives and Breathes

From the Water's Flow and the Wind's Breeze

From the Fire's glow to the Mountain's Tower

May you encircle them all with your great Power

Above and Below, You Encircle and Embrace

May I forever learn and live in your Grace

May I connect to your Divinity

May I grow in your realm of Infinity

May you forever the elements Unite

In Perfect Trust and Love and Light

Forever so May it Be

In Perfect Love and Harmony

Blessed Be

Elemental Call

Guardians of the Watchtowers, Elements of Earth

Bringers of Life that creates our Birth

Come now to join us in our sacred Rite!

We welcome thee to our circle this Night

East, I call you of Air and Breath

Blow your winds of Life and Death

Your voice is borne on the leaves of the Trees

Come now and join us, this I ask of Thee

South, I call you of Heat and Fire

The Cleansing flame of our Desire

Your beauty is seen in the heart of the Flame

Come now and join us, we are the Same

West, I call you of Water and Tide

As you rush forth, none can Hide

By the pull of the moon you rise and Fall

Come now and join us, Life giver of All

North, I call you of Earth, our Home

You sustain Life upon you where we Roam

You bring us stability, grounding and Birth

Come now and joins us of the rich moist Earth

Akasha, Great Spirit that binds all Four

Making the fifth, thee we Adore

Come now and join us, the circle is Cast

Made in Light and built to Last

As we humbly stand Thee

We honour thy Love and Harmony

In Love and Light... So Mote it Be!

Of the Elements

Of the cleansing rains that fall upon Me

Of the tides that whirl all around Me

Of the winds fury that rages through Me

Of the burning flame from the dragon's Breath

Of the earth's turn that brings life and Death

Of creation's dawn from which time Flows

Of the moonlit skies and the stars that Glow

Of thy peace and calm and Serenity

Of thy love and trust and Harmony

Of the web thou weaves spun in Light

Of the gift of day and the gift of Night

Of the wheel that turns upon a Season

Of the path we walk with rhyme and Reason

Of all that I am and ever shall Be

May I walk with Thee

In thy Blessed Harmony

So Mote it Be!

The Seeker

By the ancient stars, I seek wisdom and Clarity

By the tides that break, I seek peace and Serenity

By the fire's light, I see strength and Might

By the Earth's soil, I seek stability and Sight

By Akasha that binds, I seek perfect Harmony

By the circle cast, I seek thy sacred Purity

By the power that lasts, I seek the truth in all Things

By the spirit inside, I seek to fly on your Wings

By the dragon's breath, I seek your ancient Fire

By the magickal fae, I seek your mystic Desire

By the Lady's bright, I seek you above and Below

By the Lord of the tree, I seek your Ancient Glow

By the rock and stone, I seek your Solidity

By the Lord and Lady, Blessed Be!

John Awen

Blessings to you.

I am 44 years old and without realising, I have always been walking a Pagan path. I decided to label myself as a Druid around 3 years ago, it connected with me deeply and gave me the answers to so many questions I had been seeking. I follow the Druid path because it shows a way, an older way and one that I hold dear to myself.

However, I have my own interpretation of a lot of my beliefs and I also let other faiths and traditions have a bearing on my life.

Whatever path you may follow, I believe we should not remain too strict. Many other traditions have so much to offer and teach us and for me, that's the whole point of being here, to learn, share, grow on all levels and to find contentedness and comfort in who we are and all we are trying to attain and become.

After all, we are all connected and I don't think we should dismiss anything until we actually know more about it. We are all infinite beings and to dismiss certain items, is similar to clipping your own wings.

Thank-you so much for taking the time to read this book and I sincerely hope you enjoy it and if it can help you in any way, then that's great.

Another reason why we are all here, to help one another, comfort and console in times of need and hurt and with the balance, to enjoy the times of great laughter and joy.

I would like to take this opportunity to say a massive 'thank-you,' to my wonderful partner Jhyenan, for all her love, support and guidance, without her this book probably would not be. Can I also thank Fiona and Laura for their beautiful writings,

They are two beautiful people and so inspirational, true friends and always will be.

Uniting as One

For many of us, through our lives, we have felt different, maybe even ostracised, whether that's by others, or even by ourselves. Having spoken to many spiritual people from various faiths and traditions.

The feelings of being different from an early age are very common. It does seem very relevant, that through our lives, a lot of us were almost loners, spending time with animals and in nature, this has had such a bearing on who we have become now and it is by no coincidence that many of us are connecting up with like-minded people now, almost like a tribing together and uniting as one.

It's almost as if, all our lives we have been waiting for something, even though we just ambled along and done what we have, it's as if we were all waiting for a drive to start us off. A recognition, the spark to push us all on.

Obviously, as younger people, we didn't understand about spirituality and many of us would not have even heard the word, or if we had, would not have understood what it meant, we just knew we felt and seemed different to others and to the normal run of life.

I believe totally, that so many of us now are forming connections and friendships that will last lifetimes and if the truth be known, these are friendships that were formed in our previous lifetimes. I also believe this is why we are all connecting up now, it's as if we have been waiting patiently for our friends and kin that we knew would turn up eventually, we just didn't know when.

Spirituality, I believe, is the driving force behind it all, the connections we are all forming now and it's what pushes us all on each day. It's as if we are all coming to fruition together, a realisation of oneself and of others.

A time to grow together, to link up and share what we have and to all step up another level together and as one.

On the other side of it, it can also be a time when some people, whoever they may be, might not be able to, or even want to evolve.

This can be hard, as we then have to make the decision to, in a sense to almost wave goodbye to others, friends, family, who knows. Basically, do we move on as spiritual beings, or do we decide to clip our wings and stay as we are, thus denying our inner self the chance of learning and growth on all levels?

In all this, there is great comfort knowing that we are all on a journey together and if we share, help and love our fellow man, we can achieve so many things together.

We are all infinite beings and if we all come together as one, we can grow so much, learn so much and in turn, anything becomes possible.

Understanding and Accepting Ourselves

What is it we are all seeking? Well, there's a million dollar question. Forget all the ownership of materialistic items, the house, car, new television and such like.

What we are all really seeking is the connection to ourselves, the key to unlock what is contained within us all. We are all stumbling along this path of life, there are the smooth surfaces and then, ultimately, there are the bumpy parts.

None of us know where we are heading, we just have to use the tools we are given and have adapted ourselves, to suit each situation that may and will invariably rise. We are all on a quest in this life, the thing is, we do not and cannot know or even start to comprehend exactly what that quest is.

Personally, I totally believe that we are all here to find ourselves first, then and only then can we really start to discover what life and creation is really all about.

Firstly we have to know us, we have to become aware of who we really are, we have to, not only like ourselves, but we have to truly love the person we are. We have to understand that all that lies within has shaped and molded who we are and will ultimately become.

If we look back and see certain parts of our own being that we do not really like, we have to face them and understand that it was all part of our path, our learning curve and part of who we have become.

We should see all our failings and shortfalls as our journey, learn from them and see them as a blessing for the recognition of who we are now, learn from them and see them as part of the celestial balance of all that is and the perfect balance in life, to which we are all trying to attain. Once we confront these darker places, we can understand ourselves and know that none of us are ever infallible, we are just doing what we thought, or believed to be right at that time.

It's a very hard and complex lesson to undertake and certainly to understand.

None of us, as humans, ever want to admit or even face our shortcomings, but as spiritual beings and to evolve, we have to. admit, work on and then move on and away from these darker recesses of ourselves.

We have to nurture the untamed beast within and we should

calm and nurture our restless souls. Without doing this, we simply cannot and will not evolve to move on, not on any level, physically, mentally, or spiritually.

If we can achieve this, then as spiritual beings, we can and will ultimately move on. Within this understanding of ourselves, we are then free to share our faults with the wider world and then in turn, we can share what we have learnt and hopefully pass on the knowledge which we have learnt, ultimately helping another.

I believe this is a major step in becoming empathic and feeling the pains, troubles and plights of others. After all, this is all part of the evolution process of the inner self and the being in which our spirit wants us to become.

Once we can mirror image ourselves and truly love the whole person and being which we are, then we can start to resonate outwardly to others, this in turn, can be an example and maybe a guide to our fellow man.

Once and if we can become totally happy in our own skin, we can truly help and support others on their paths, which we can only really do, if we have reached a greater understanding of the failings of mankind. We can reach a happy medium and know that none of us are perfect and nor should we want to be. We just have to learn,

understand, accept and move on to the next level.

Trees

The wind gently wafts through the trees; the leaves rustle against each other.

The branches gently sway to and fro, as if caressing one another. The movement is sporadic, yet captivating and hypnotic.

These great old trees have stood the test of time; they hold much knowledge and wisdom. In full bloom they are absolutely beautiful, stunning and so majestic.

They have witnessed so much and hold many secrets. In the autumn time, they shed their leaves and get ready to withstand the coldness of winter.

They take on another form once the leaves have dropped, like a skeleton, they are still inviting and their nakedness is there for all to see.

A retreat, and a time of slumber and renewal. Almost a time of stasis befalls them, awaiting rebirth and fruition, newness and growth. These grand trees constantly cleanse. They purify the air that we breathe, always helping, assisting and giving out new life to us, with the clean air they exude for and to us.

When they shed their branches, we can gather them, collect and burn them. They warm us and we can cook from the heat they give out.

Medicines can be extracted from the bark, the sap, the roots, the leaves and berries. Foodstuffs can be harvested also.

A constant cycle of growth, death and rebirth, one we can all see each day, right in front of us.

These grand old trees are always there in their beauty. Offering and giving life, warmth, and shelter and healing. They never ask for anything in return, just always giving.

Honour the trees; listen to them, as they hold the knowledge of all creation.

Commune with them, touch and feel them often. Walk in and amongst them. Take the time to give thanks for all they provide us with and honour them totally.

Old Knobbly (An Ancient Oak, Essex)
Photo by John Awen

The Big Bang theory or Not?

All of us throughout our lives have and will many times wonder how we and the planets came into existence. Gazing up at the night sky always inspires us, the infinity of it all and will jog our subconscious beings into wondering why and how everything that is became.

As a child forced into the Christian Sunday school, even at a young age, the parable of a god creating everything in six days and resting on the seventh never felt right or sat well with me and I never believed it. What I am about to say is my own interpretation of how I think all the world and universe came into being. Even though a lot of which I will mention is being researched now and scientist across the world are working on the theory.

So Here I go, opening up another Pandora's box.

I consider that before it all started there was just blackness, absolutely no light, just nothingness and darkness.

I do believe however, that there would have been energy, not taking form, because form wouldn't have been possible, but energy in and contained within the darkness. I like to personally think that a God and Goddess, like a yin and yang being, two within one, were contained within an energy consciousness. Magic and Science can run side by side, and one complements the other.

Therefore, I like to think that the energy consciousness of the God and Goddess combined somehow implemented would and could be described as the big bang theory causing energy to take solid form causing matter to be created.

Scientist in Switzerland and France over the last few years at CERN, have and are still working on the Higgs-Bowson Particle, which is also being labelled as "the god particle."

This particle, recently discovered via the "Hadron Collider," gives energy its mass. So now we are taking it one step further from what I have always believed about the energy held in the planet to start with, this "god particle", as it's called can now help and assist energy to take various form. Without this particle, nothing could exist. This particle is responsible for every form that we can view, see, feel and touch contained within the whole universe. So let's take it back a step now, as I said earlier, I always believed there was darkness, but there was energy contained within a God and Goddess consciousness, but nothing was formed or could be.

Now we can intrinsically know that with this scientific discovery, basically, we can have the big bang theory, where worlds are created. Another creation myth of the Celtic Path of which I follow calls the creation the Oran Mor, The Great Melody. Where basically there was nothingness, apart from water, until a subtle harmony began, like a music vibration and as it gathered its energy, it broke out into a huge crescendo forming all life and all of creation. This harmony still continues now and is the heartbeat and pulse contained within every living thing.

This is the vibration at which attunement and connection can be felt, recognised and achieved. Could this be the song of the Goddess? Which is known as the pulse of the Earth.

As I said earlier, I never believed other interpretations of creation, I had my own and now the Higgs-Bowson Particle has made me realise that I don't think I was too far off. As with anything, it's open to interpretations. This is my interpretation of it alone with proven science and for me this works.

Spirituality

To live life to the full, surely is the reason we are all here to partake and be an integral part of creation and life as a whole. We are all spiritual beings having a human existence... we do not have to achieve spirituality, it is already in us and we are a part of it... We just need to merely re-attune ourselves, our minds and our thought process....Once we realise this, we open up the floodgates to the celestial web, which links us and all life that has been, is now and will be...Our thoughts are new to this life and this body in which we inhabit and unfortunately our inner and true senses get dampened down, mainly due to societies oppression and not wanting free thinking beings walking around... No way do the so called powers that be want free thinking people.

I mean we would simply not stand for the regime they are trying to create and install upon us all, everything would be questioned by us and the power they attempt to exert upon us all would simply diminish and fade, then where would they be ? So in reality, it's in all of our best interests, to open up our minds and the minds of others, to create a more harmonious planet and universe... One in which we can all walk around freely expressing ourselves and trying to create a united and joyous life and existence, not just for us, but for the planet and all of life upon it, because everything is linked so intrinsically to all that is, everything we do and all we undertake has repercussions on every level and aspect of our lives and our whole being.

We are all physical, mental and spiritual beings, so it therefore goes without saying that anything we do in our physical body, will have a knock on effect, good or bad to our mental and spiritual selves and vice-versa. The bigger picture is crucial in all of our daily lives and we have to always look at the positive effects and also the negative ones, each action and motion is going to have upon us, each other and the world as a whole.

This can take lifetimes to achieve and no doubt we have all achieved it in a previous life here, but now we have to re-learn it, tap into it and put it into action. Once we can grasp this idea, then we can call upon our inner and older self, spirit around us and the akashic records for help and solutions and answers when needed, to simply heighten and enlighten ourselves and other people around.

Our minds are the most complex and powerful tool we have and we don't use a quarter of them. The mind can hold and has infinite knowledge, creation and ideas. All these are connected to the web of life, as all beings are. If we can attune ourselves to higher levels of belief and better ways to live, then surely we are increasing our spiritual beings, in turn this is better for our mental and physical selves and then in turn again, better for all life and creation, the world and universe as a whole.

Glastonbury Tor, picture taken by John Awen

Self Realisation

A time of self-realisation befalls us. A time when we can often question our whole being, why we are here, what is the point and what's going to happen next? These feelings and internal questions can rear their head at any time of our lives.

If we ignore these questions, we are going into self-denial and maybe even just going along for the ride and being complacent. As spiritual beings, it's natural to question and wonder what may befall us. This journey we are on is a sacred and very delicate path, a path of learning, understanding and acknowledging all of creation. We will never know all the answers, if we did, we wouldn't be here now.

To question our own self is a great start and a good way of becoming a better person and this, in turn can then spur and lead us on to seek out answers that we can only get, if we become part of all that is and in doing so, we can then link up to the celestial web of immortality and then tap into the akashic records, which, for me, is the holy grail we are all seeking anyway. Imagine a massive data base where there are all the answers to all the questions on anything, past, present and future. This is the infinite source of knowledge and wisdom and it's available to every one of us, we just have to seek honour and become attuned and it's all there for us.

Once we can walk with ourselves, be loving, true, generous, empathic and understanding, then the spiritual beings which we are, can flow freely and all the knowledge of all that ever was, is and will be in the future, is all there for us to reach into, know and share.

Rekindle the Fire

The feeling of utter and total peace and calmness resides within us all. The key to our existence and happiness is to unlock it. From birth we are conditioned. We are spoon fed clutter illusional stuff, which we are told will make us better people and help in our existence. The society which we are all a part of, no matter how much we try not to be, does and will control all of us throughout our lives, it's virtually impossible to not be drawn into societies throws, however hard we try, plus the fact that no man can be an island.

As people we all have our homes, our shelters, family and friends, where we can be ourselves and feel comfortable and that is the ultimate key to it all. Finding ourselves, looking within and unlocking the real you, that lies within. It's not about conforming, it's not about rebelling, it's simply about becoming, and embracing the spirit inside, nurturing it, understanding it, flourishing and evolving with the deep meaningful and soulful being inside us all Many, many lifetimes, this evolution of oneself has been forming and coming into fruition. We simply can't and mustn't deny it now.

The drumbeat that resides in all creation, the "Oran mor" that bought and gave all life form and being, is rising like a crescendo now, you can feel it, it stirs your every waking moment. It's the beauty all around, the birdsong, the trees and flowers, the sun and moon, the stars in the night sky.

Your partner and loved ones all around and the memories of others passed on.From birth, we re-awaken the spirit, the awe and wonderment of all sights, smells, tastes, the feel of all around, you must remember it, we all do.

Then society steps in, reconditions us and we all become blinkered and almost blind to the beauty all around and dumbed down on our other senses. Awaken all that lays within you, push the switch again and turn the power back on. Bring back to life your all seeing inner self and see it through your inner child's eyes again.To not do this, to not really see and appreciate all around, is denying your whole being and existence, physically, mentally and spiritually. Like a snub to the creation and God and Goddess that put us here.

It's no better than throwing it all back in their faces. We are all infinite beings, on so many levels. Re-kindle the fire, light and truth inside you and become everything you ever dreamed of and more.

Why Druidry?

I am often asked as a Druid, to explain what a Druid is and my beliefs, I often retract from this question and turn it around to not what, but simply why?

Ever since I can remember I have loved and felt at home, out and about in the woods, fields, sitting by rivers and just soaking up and communing with the great outdoors.

For me personally, I always feel so free and able to express myself when I am outside and not indoors. I have always enjoyed walking and just enjoying all that this beautiful world has to offer. We can let our minds soar, our thoughts wander, we can be healed and it's so good for us physically, mentally and spiritually when we go outside. I have often just sat under trees that speak to me, I talk to the flowers, trees, animals, the stars, the elements and everything around. Many times when I have had problems, as we all do, they seem to fade and almost become irrelevant when I am outside. There is no oppression, we can be who we are and we can see and view the world and universe as its meant to be seen, basically we become more and truly connected with all that is.

Spirit, nature as a whole and our ancestors can listen and talk back to us, we can relay messages and achieve a greater and higher understanding, we are able to tap in to source and the holy grail, which to me is the akashic records, if we just simply connect with our inner selves, thus increasing our spirituality and in turn connecting to all of creation. Once we can do this, we can all become at one, both with ourselves, others and all that is.I know a lot of you will all be feeling you have connected with the universe and you may be treading another belief ,faith or religion and yes, many other faiths work and can achieve the same, so again 'Why' Druidry? As a Druid, I like and always have wanted to learn as much about everything that I can.

I see my mind as a sponge and want and need to soak up all the information and intricate workings, that I can. I personally believe this is the reason we are all here, to learn, share and pass on as much knowledge and wisdom as we can. We have all been here before and learnt it, we just have to now, learn it again and maybe a different path, simply because each time we come here, we have lessons to learn and once we can shake off the restrictive blinkers, which the modern day society inflicts upon us all, we can realise an infinite journey of the mind and soul, then we can begin our own personal journey of evolution of the self.

I believe we should all take a step back, to move forward, looking at the bigger picture of all things.

We should train our minds to not judge, to not jump to conclusions. We should just mentally sit back and ask ourselves, why? As spiritual beings all having a human existence this is so vital to allow our bodies physically, mentally and spiritually to move on and maybe in doing this, we can become cleaner in all we do and undertake...Almost like watching the night sky, we are looking at the whole situation, it's as if we can see all the intricacies and inner workings...It's no good just watching a segment and then making a sudden rash choice or decision based on that, we simply have to look at it all, then we may be able to see, where, when, how, who and why we are all here? We may never know all of this, but on our journey on and through this amazing life, if we can achieve some of this, then surely we are on our way to becoming the people we want to and the change we would all like to be and bring about in the world today. So, as I said earlier for me, it's not what is Druidry, its simply why?

Brightest of blessings.

Nature or Nurture?

Nature and nurture. Fight or flight? As with all creation, there is a balance, there has to be. Without this sacred balance, we simply would not and could not be. Dark and light, love and hate, hot and cold, etc. When we look at all aspects of creation, there is always a male/female side as well, some may seem more dominant, but as with the ying & yang, it does balance itself out, it has to, otherwise the scales would be tipped in the favour of one and all that is precious could not be.

Creation has in abundance this precious balance worked out, basically so that everything can co-exist and harmonise each other. When we look at ourselves in the male and female roles, a lot of the time the roles, over the millennia have been clearly defined...The male can be interpreted as the strong hunter/gatherer, while the female role has and can be viewed as the child bearer and home maker....Society over the last few decades has tried to put a different take on this, simply by giving woman the opportunity to take on more male orientated roles, nothing wrong in that at all...Whether we are male, or female, we have the other gender inside us all anyway, simply to have balance, without this, I don't believe we could be as creative as we are and we couldn't be as empathic as we are either.

Each and every day, we all call upon our other sides, intentionally or not, we do. Each of us is in a body vessel and outwardly, we look either male or female. Due to the fact that the inner self is made up totally of energy, our life force can take the feelings and persona of the other role, male/female, thus allowing us to communicate on all levels and to stay in touch with our male/female counterparts and our inner selves.

To nature and nurture is seen as the feminine aspect on the whole, this can be construed by the fact that woman are life givers, they have babies, they feed them and they have a bond everlasting with their children. The fight or flight aspect is down to the man, the male counterpart of the woman. To be the provider of food, warmth and years ago, to go into battle to prove his masculinity and strength.

Personally, I believe, woman are more intuitive than males are, they see and view this world and other realms differently, woman can be so much more empathic than men can, it's one of their traits.

To be with a partner is an amazing gift, a sacred and very precious journey into the unknown. To have this gift with your soul mate, your one true love is even more of a gift and a true blessing. A lot of people, unfortunately never experience this, but if you do, your feelings, emotions, values and your whole perception is heightened. To achieve this unity is what we are all striving and looking for. Our minds want it and our inner being and life force so long for it, it's why we are here in the first place.

To achieve the one true partnership with that special person is heightening our beings on all levels, physically, mentally and spiritually. If we can achieve this, then I believe the parts we play, in our male and female forms come to fruition as well.

The female role, is to bring and help the male achieve his full potential spiritually, without the female guidance and input, I do not believe this can be achieved. The male role in this, is to protect the woman while she walks this earth and to attain his spirituality while they walk hand in hand together. The balance is in perfect harmony then and if you take or remove either, it simply cannot and will not be.

The Collective

As a collective of bodies, humanity and peoples thought patterns and minds are starting to change rapidly at the moment. I call it waking up and basically that's what it is. For too long now, we have all just gone along and accepted what society tells us, this is partly due to peer pressures and also because it's a lot easier to not ask questions which may rock the boat.

Oppression has been inflicted on us all since birth. We do manage to escape this to a certain degree, as young toddlers and children we simply learn as we grow, unfortunately though when we start school, this learning process diminishes rapidly and being 'taught,' comes into force. The difference there is because as humans we have a burning desire to learn, it's a natural instinct and part of all that is, a natural way to progress and a big part of the cycle of life and universe.

Being 'taught,' is a way to subtly dampen down this natural process and basically get people to comply and condition them, thus installing subtle fear on many levels and then in turn we all remain duped, silent and will not question the authorities simply because fear has been installed and this in turn brings about a control from the so called powers that be.

It is human nature to question things and once we realise there is so much more to life, than just being part of the system, it is so much easier to break those oppressive chains and stand on your own to ask why are we allowing this to happen and surely life is about so much more than this?

I have seen and witnessed over the last few years, almost a mass union and joining together of like-minded people breaking away from societies shackles and simply saying, this is not right, there is a better way of life.

It is a time of realisation on all levels, mentally, physically and spiritually, more and more people are now fed up and yearn for a massive cleansing of the universe and mankind as a whole.

Obviously, we are all on different levels of learning and we walk and tread a multitude of varying paths, but we are finding and sharing so much more common ground now and this is the collective consciousness of mankind and the celestial web of all things, kicking into gear and pushing forward as a unit and together.

We may have to wave goodbye to some friends and people on this journey, this can be hard to do and to cope with, but advancement of the self and as a whole, has to take priority and we have to progress on all levels when we can, otherwise you are simply denying yourself and others the chance of a better life. Personally, I believe and am sure this is the reason so many strong bonds, ties and friendships are being forged now, even with people we haven't actually met yet. It's the old saying, light attracts light and vice versa. Together we can all walk as one and step up a gear together and we will reach a better place and a more loving existence and world will all be revealed and prevail to us all.

Blessings.

Path to Paganism

From about the age of seven until about the age of ten, I was forced to attend Church of England Sunday school. To say I was reluctant would have been an understatement. I remember distinctly, even at a young age, churches just seemed to be too oppressive, even though I didn't know fully what they stood for. Still, off I went each Sunday to learn about this book called the Bible and the teachings in it. I remember clearly to this day, sitting down with the other children and being read what I would now call parables, stories then. As if it was yesterday, I can clearly remember sticking my hand up constantly several times each Sunday and each week thereafter asking, how and why these so called miracles could happen. This probably didn't stand me in good stead with the Sunday school teacher as after several weeks even with my hand waving frantically in the air, I was readily being ignored.

I had then and still have an enquiring mind and will not settle for just being told. I like to find out all of the answers so I am able to weigh it out for myself, basically I want to know the truth about it or my perspective of the truth, which can vary from person to person.

I admit now and have to both my parents since, that I did abscond for about the last year of this and I found at these times, even at the age of nine and ten, walking through woods, touching trees and sitting under them, wildlife spotting and watching the seasons change and also enjoying being outside in all the elements.

Looking back now, I can see that I have always been of pagan belief, I just did not know that then, but even then, this was going to stand me in good stead and eventually place me on my journey to becoming a Druid. I have over the years looked into several different beliefs/faiths, and was always left asking more and more questions and not feeling satisfied with their portrayal of that belief/religion. It was only upon researching about Druid/Druidry, that I realised for me personally this is the one belief that totally ticked every single box.

I decided about two years ago to label myself a druid and walk this earthly path. For me, it totally encapsulates all that has been, all that is now and all that will be. Be it, in reach, up in the sky and out of reach, in other realms and many things we cannot even perceive to understand, but warms a deep rooted core and sparks a fire inside me.

To not only breathe the air, but to taste it, to not only hear the bird sound, but truly listen to it, to watch the buds come on the trees and the seasons change, to stand freezing cold and soaked to the skin on a stormy day or night. To raise your hands in the air, to exhale and to feel the spirit that dwells within.

To be comforted by the spirit, when you're feeling lonely. To feel warm when you know you're cold. To look at the bigger picture and to just be aware of all that is. There is so much more to being a druid and none of us should ever stop learning. This for me personally is the base and the glue of what being a druid is about and I am so grateful to be walking this path and treading along this journey. So mote it be!

Journey of Discovery

From an early age, we all are on a journey of discovery, an unknown path of which none of us know what our journey will reveal, where we are heading and what we will find, basically we are all on a magical mystery tour. A journey with highs and lows, sheer joy, despair, love, hurt and many other wondrous feelings.

As we grow, we can and invariably do, take on our parents/guardians and mentors viewpoints and understandings of different situations. This is so easily done as we absorb, consciously and subconsciously peoples energies, we then can at times take them on as our own thoughts and views.

As we proceed through and on our journey, our views can and ultimately do change and the viewpoints we have, that seem set in stone have to and will change for each given situation.

A viewpoint we have, has to be flexible, simply because each situation has total difference and two situations are never the same. We have to view each encounter and see it on its own merits, basically this is life experience and something we should all arrive at.

Life is not and can never be black and white, it's just not that way and I for one am so very glad that it's not that way. Having a total and clear understanding of life and different dilemmas, as they unfold is paramount to our personal growth on all levels, it's basically teaching yourself and learning to view the bigger and whole picture of all that is. This is crucial to becoming empathic and non-judgmental, which none of us should be. In doing this, we are drawing on our own experiences of life situations, our memories, our past experiences and the collective unconscious.

To become an integral part of creation and life as a whole, we have to de-clutter our minds, basically empty the glass and then refill it with our own views, interpretations and takes on various situations. Without doing this, we cannot move forward and unfortunately, we will only view the world in a two dimensional state, instead of the four dimensions we are supposed to view it in. Become the real you and see the different and beautiful colours and all the varying shades in between.

Intergration

From the moment we are born, we are constantly integrating with the world around us. Our Mothers are usually the first person we integrate with, as we have already bonded with them from inside the womb. Once we are born, we have the ability to see exactly six inches, which is the distance from breast to face, therefore we can see our Mums face and this is where recognition and integration begins in this world.

From this moment on, we constantly are integrating, adapting and learning how to connect, with other people, animals and the world around us, also our inner selves. This trait is with us all our lives, through schooling, teenage years and right through our adult lives. Social acceptance plays a major part in all of this, as it has to.We want to be accepted, we have the need all of our lives, to 'fit in ' and in our younger years, this can inevitably play a major part of how we evolve and the type of person we turn out to be. Peer pressure plays a massive part in all of this, as life is a learning curve and we want and need to be accepted.

Our teenage years are probably the most vulnerable time for the majority of us, as there are so many different groups of people, which can influence us greatly, basically as we are still finding our feet and still do not know who we really are.

We therefore adapt and frequently change the person we really are, almost as if we are trying on various personas, until we can all ultimately find 'us' and become who we truly are. Connecting with all around, creation as a whole and our own inner self is crucial in all of this, we may want and need to fit in with others and can often appear in various guises to do this, which really is all part of the finding of our true selves and liking the person inside, from this point onwards in life, then we can actually stand alone, be happy with who we are and evolve and strengthen the real us. You can liken this to the caterpillar and the various stages of its growth and to its ultimate destination of the butterfly. Once we can actually connect and become who we truly are inside, we can then like us and evolve in the different stages of who we are.

This evolving comes physically, mentally and spiritually. We gain strength, wisdom and a plethora of other attributes, all of which ultimately come from the self-realisation of who we really are. Once we can stand alone and know this, the world opens up, linking us to source, spirit and the collective unconscious, which basically is the celestial web and the intrinsical source of all that is. If we can attain this, then we have flourished and grown immensely and ultimately, I believe achieved what is, the reason we are all here in the first place. Unfortunately, not all beings can achieve this. This is the reason we often have various factions and splinter groups. Through all walks of life there will always be people that don't live their life truthfully; they merely exist on the peripherals of existence.

Social outcasts, some of their own choosing and others who just have not learnt and may not have the capability and various skills, to integrate with others and the world as a whole. For me personally it's all about becoming the real me, learning, sharing, helping, loving and only doing good to others and creation as a whole. Evolving and connecting with all that is and all that ever will be and integrating on all levels.

Blessings.

Free Thinking

From the earliest appearance by mankind on this planet, we have had to constantly think and work to achieve even the most basic tasks. Catching and growing our own food. Lighting our homes and cooking a meal had to be done, but from the time early man awoke, he had to fetch and carry wood, catch and collect the food. It was a constant battle to survive and generally to stay alive, it would have been hard no doubt about it.

As a society now, most of us don't have to think at all. We go round pressing buttons, to turn a light on, boil water and cook, we do not have to think at all to achieve any of this, we just press and go. Surely and it has to be, that this simplistic lifestyle, has to have a massive knock on effect to us and it certainly has. As a species we have become dumbed down, simply because we don't have to think anymore.

We, at home, choose not to have a television and wouldn't want one, but how many of you watch programs and adverts that force feed you total rubbish. They tell you what they want you to know and no more. The adverts almost tell you what to buy in your weekly shopping. How many of you have been out and bought your shopping, returned home and unpacked it and wondered why on earth you purchased some of the stuff you have?

Clever marketing and almost an hypnotic effect in the way it happens. Just before an advert comes on, some programs even tell you when you can go and make a drink, what's all that about? It's a crazy world and in doing this, the whole system and marketing strategy is keeping you from free thinking and keeping us all lethargic and dumbed down.

If you think and I mean really think about this, it's all about controlling the masses and society as a whole. If we all attuned ourselves, physically, mentally and especially spiritually, we would all see this for the illusion and total farce that it is.

From the time we awake in the morning, until we retire at the end of the day, we are all being controlled, manipulated and force fed total rubbish on all levels. This is simply to keep us all conforming and a part of the system. Try to step outside of the box, walk within nature and become a part of the true world. Question everything and try not to fall in line. I am not saying go against everything, I am just saying, take a look outside of the box and feel, become and embrace the true and real person that lies inside you. We are all capable of so much more, it's infinite. Give it a go.

Shake off societies blinkers and constraints and just become who you were meant to be, a free thinking individual.

Footprints

From the earliest time that we, the species of man arrived on this planet, there has been a total balance. Mankind, from the earliest times, worked with and alongside the natural balance that resides and exists in all creation. They woke when it became light and retired to sleep when it got dark. Animals were hunted for food, clothing and bedding and fires were lit to cook upon, for protection and to keep warm.

Nature and the balance within, was worked with totally and this carried on for thousands of years and I believe, even though it would have been extremely hard and that's only because our conception of life like that from our comfy homes makes it seem so, it would have been a more fulfilling existence and one that kept everything in sync with how it is meant to be.

Since the start of the industrial revolution, back in the late 1800's, mankind has forced itself upon this beautiful planet. There have been tens of thousands of miles of woodland destroyed and replaced with cities, towns and other monstrous creations. Rivers have been re-routed and so many have been totally eradicated for so called gain. Natural resources have been raped and some are now gone forever, never to be replaced.

Artificial lighting is now used everywhere to control the times we can do and create things. Genetically modified people, crops, insects are now being manufactured, some, simply because we can and others because we have totally destroyed the natural environment in which they live. I know that mankind in itself has grown a lot, exploded really, but so many of these changes are and have proved totally pointless. The natural ying & yang of all life and creation has and is now being destroyed and taken away forever and to me and if you all really think about it and become empathic towards our beautiful planet, you can see and feel how utterly devastating all this truly is.

Only within the last 150 – 200 years has this happened and apart from mankind's greed and longing to be in control of everything, I cannot find an answer to it. Total rape and pillage seems to be the driving force of many of the world's so called governing bodies. To be in control and to ultimately gain control of the masses, us basically, that is the order of the day.

As a society, we are so wasteful, we really are. From the foodstuffs we eat, the packaging used, the items we have in our homes, the vehicles we drive, fuel we burn, we all just use and if it's broken, or slightly damaged, we simply throw it away and buy another one.

Even as recent as the 1940's & 50's, people were being encouraged to 'make do & mend,' why has this changed?

Respect seems to be a word we don't hear anymore, respect for our hard earned money, we just keep earning it and buying the latest goods to be marketed and inflicted upon us. Consumerism has gone crazy, so many people just buy, simply because they can and are made to feel they should.

Respect for others and ultimately ourselves. All these virtues seem, somewhere along the line, to have gotten lost in mankind's bid to possess and rule the planet.

We, as a race should be reverting back to the ways of our ancestors, forget all the latest gadgets, forget all the GM crops and other modified stuffs, start living in harmony and balance with creation and the world as a whole. We must all strive to evolve and in doing this, we should all be showing respect for this beautiful place we all call home.

Work with and alongside her, let her grow her trees, flow her rivers and generally bare her fruits and animals naturally. None of us have the right to damage and cause willful destruction of this sacred place. We are the guardians and caretakers of this earth and we will ultimately pass it on to our children, what state will it be in then ?

We must all strive to become the change we want to see, however small you may think it is, be that change you want to happen. Start honouring and working with and alongside the natural balance in all life, species and the world as a whole. Leave behind only memories and footprints.

Connections

No matter where in the world we live, the sun will rise and set, the moon will wax and wane, creation is abundant, will heal us all, warm, guide and inspire us. We are all one, we are all connected. Some say we are all connected by seven degrees, forget all that, we are all the same and we are from the same source. Our earthly parents are and will be different, we all have different Mothers and Fathers, but ultimately we are the same and we are born of and from the one same source.

As we tread our paths and see and view the bigger picture, it slowly becomes clear just how close and intrinsically linked we all truly are. Just pick up a handful of sand. You can see different shapes, colourings and markings. We are all like those grains of sand, all different, but ultimately the same.

The ocean tide will wash, cleanse and move the grains of sand about, weakening parts of the beach they are all forming, yet strengthening other parts. Compare yourselves with that beach. Life can wash over us. Cleansing, healing, moving us about and connecting us all with other grains of sand, i.e. other people and like-minded souls, friends, brothers and sisters. We can all get and invariably do, get washed away from time to time, we end up in unfamiliar and uncertain places and with people we do not know. This can seem unsettling and unnerving.

If we just flip those feelings over and view it like a grain of sand, wherever we are and travel to, we are always with our kin, our friends and family, simply because we are all one and the same.

The unseen celestial web of all that has been, is now and will be, enshrouds us all. Like a massive invisible mesh that covers this whole planet, each realm and all the other worlds in their entirety. Therefore, we are all connected, similar to a huge jigsaw puzzle, all the pieces have a place, they fit but, if you take away just one small piece of that puzzle, it's all incomplete and simply will not work.

We are all on our different paths, none of us know where these paths will ultimately lead us to, nor should we want to know. It's all about enjoying this special and very sacred journey.

Just like the grains of sand, we are all different and with each passing tide, we can get moved, we change and we can evolve.

No matter how much we go through, we are all part of all that is and we all have a part to play within the grand scheme of things.

We are all one, connected to each other and all that is. Our past lives, this life and our future lives as well. A total oneness with each other and the universe and creation as a whole.

Be Proud

We have all heard the phrase, 'time of our lives.' This is this moment and the life we are leading now and at this moment. It has taken us all our lives to reach this point in time.

We have conquered and overcome many things to reach here now. Joy, love, pain, and many other emotions and trials. All these feelings have shaped us and molded us into the very person you see looking back at you from the mirror.

Smile back at yourself, you are strong and have journeyed much, you are still here and all that has happened and all that you have gone through, has taught you a lot, made you wiser and put you just where you stand today.

Be proud of who you are, stand strong and carry on.
The past is the past, the future is uncertain, but what really matters and counts is the now. Live it totally and embrace it with your whole being.

So long as you walk into each new day with love and purity in your heart and good intention in your mind, you can hold your head up high. Be proud of your journey so far and who it has made you.

Ancestors

We are the ancestors of tomorrow. During our lives, we inhabit and visit various places, some of these places are already familiar to us, we feel as if we know the surroundings and have been there before. This is because we have, just in another body vessel and in a previous existence.

We have walked these and other lands before, it's just our minds, as they are now, do not remember them.Our souls do, a kind of re-awakening of the spirit and the heartbeat that dwells and beats within all of us. This is the energy/source/spirit that exists throughout time and remains with us throughout all our lives and for eternity.

We can and often do awaken the spirit and connect with people, places, sights and smells, this is the point when we are truly awakened inside and do visit the other side of the veil, the other realm, where our ancestors reside. We are todays ancestors also. Our past lives mean that when we think of our ancestors, we are linking and touching ourselves, our ancestors are us. Energy, which we are all made up of, never dies, I believe, it just goes to the Summer lands to rest, restore and rejuvenate and then invariably come back, albeit in another body vessel.

We can all go off track in our lives, that's often how we learn.

We have all done things which can be detrimental to others, creation as a whole and invariably ourselves, whether it's physically, mentally or spiritually.

All these have a knock on effect anyway, so if we harm others, physically, it can affect them spiritually and vice versa. Like ripples on a pond, this can grow and basically be harmful to many others and the world.It's all about realisation, making changes, growing in all aspects, flourishing, learning and putting it all into practice. We just have to realise our wrongs, put them right and put it into action. None of us want to go through life being miserable and causing distress, on any level, it's simply not in our base make up. When we feel our ancestors with and around us, we are really feeling ourselves and this can often be the reason we feel so akin to them.

The journey of ourselves has gone on throughout millennia and will go on forever.

We are time travellers and we will continue to travel throughout time to come and for eternity, it's just we make various stops on the way, like now, we have all pulled into this station to experience another life and chapter in the story of ourselves and creation.

Baggage can get lost at stations, as it always does. If we view this baggage as our residual energy, then that is what we are leaving behind on our journeys. This is the energy we all often feel in places and connect in with and to.

It cannot always be a good feeling, sometimes it can be negative, dark, or just indifferent. As we all walk these life paths, we should all grow and evolve, on all levels.

We should honour all that is, only do positive things, help others, thus creating a more harmonious space and world in which to inhabit, live and reside in. If we can all achieve this, we are then creating a place where we will all feel more comfortable, easier and therefore, happier. We are the ancestors of tomorrow. We are yesterday's ancestors also, they are us and we are them. If we can achieve the human spirits goal of living sacred lives and honouring all life and creation, then we can rest easy, simply by knowing that we are not leaving any bad residual energy for our future selves to feel and pick up on the next time we visit this station.Leave only positivity, love, good memories.

Age and Youth

Many cultures and tribes across the world let their children grow up naturally, they take them hunting, they show them the basic life skills and pass on all the knowledge they have learnt themselves. In doing this they can hopefully pass on from generation to generation the correct and ethical way to live and then support their own family unit when the time comes. This way of learning from Father to son, Mother to daughter has been handed down through the centuries and lineage and shows how to truly respect all life and creation as a whole, taking only what is necessary to survive and causing the minimal amount of loss to mother earth.

These same cultures, Native American Indians, Inuits, Eskimo's, Aborigine's and several other localised tribes spanning all across the world honour the elders amongst them also. With old age also comes much wisdom, teachings, knowledge and much, much more. They are asked about all types of various situations and are seen as the total heads of that tribe. Problems with hunting, where to live, what to eat, medicines, child birth and a myriad of other day to day issues that need to be acted upon. Basically, nothing happens without the elders say so.

I keep asking myself why don't we live and practice this way of life? We urge and long to see our new born children take their first steps and to start talking.

Why is it then, that when they have achieved this, a lot of people (and I do not mean everyone) spend the next few years telling them to sit down and be quiet?

A lot of elderly people are also shut away in homes and it's as if they have become a burden or an embarrassment to the family unit and society as a whole. I also know of several people that care very well for their parents, aunties, uncles, etc. and do a grand job with little help .Shouldn't we be harnessing the life lessons they can share with us all, they have so much to offer, it just seems a shame to almost lock them away. Age should be embraced and so should youth. Seen through these different age gaps we can utilise the innocence of youth and totally encompass the sheer wisdom of the elderly.

I do totally understand this may not always be feasible and possible to do, what with today's modern living, but if we can all take more time and patience we can learn from both these generations of very wise and intuitive people.

We can learn so much from the young and the elderly and we can view the world around and see the bigger picture altogether. Almost like a resource, we can put it to good use and learn so much from them. Wisdom and innocence is priceless and between both, they have so much to give.

Blessings.

Armageddon

I would just like to say before you read this, that this is my interpretation, my dreams and visions of what this beautiful world and universe may turn into and what could happen. It's not all good and it's not all love and light, it cannot be, as much as I would like to see that happen, it is merely a utopian dream. Balance has to be in all creation, thus we have to have good and bad, same as we have light and dark.

The whole communications network is getting so bunged up it will eventually crash, leaving us all floundering for a while, as we all rely on mobile phones, e-mails, facebook and other communication devices. Mankind has survived for thousands of years without any of this and we will again, it's just a case of adapting. Hospitals and the whole of the NHS, as we know it now will crash and end, then we can and will revert back to the old ways, herbalists, wise woman/men and natural healing remedies.

I also envisage that before this happens, the army and other armed forces will seize power, and in turn create Marshall law, curfews will come into force, imprisonment, shootings and basically rioting will become widespread and lots of blood will inevitably be shed.

I can see the police becoming non-existent, you only have to see the way private security firms are being employed more and more to see this will happen. Money will cease and therefore become totally worthless, it will come down to creating a community in which we can live, share resources, skills, labour, food and thrive again, together as we are meant to. All fuel will become unavailable, to prevent travel, only to the armed services will this be readily available and used to try and gain control and I can see a world of either, conform to the regime, or not. I can see big glass domes, like the ones on the Eden project and a lot like the film, 'The Island.' If you are willing to conform and be told how to live, I believe this will be where you could live. A place where they force their beliefs onto you and control you totally. It would be similar to working for the system now, they would provide you with living quarters, fresh air, clothing, food and entertainment, but you would have to comply totally, otherwise you would be evicted and end up living outside of the bubble.

The pollutants they are spraying in our skies and onto all our foodstuffs, is just the start of it...They are subduing us all and attempting to create a mankind that does not question, but just follows. I know I could and would not live in such a controlled environment, it is against all my beliefs and against my natural instinct. I am now and always have been slightly different, I don't like to conform, my mind is too enquiring and I am a survivor.

Given the choice, I would take my chances living on the peripherals and on the edge of society. If this ever happens in my lifetime, I will not be in the dome. I would take my chances outside and attempt to create another way and a better understanding. Forced living can never work well, and it's totally out of balance with creation and the way we are all supposed to live.

In the end, Mother nature will put it all right and cleanse the whole planet, she always does and then peace, harmony and a newer better world could be created.

A more harmonious, natural and ethical way of life will be born again. The cycle of life continues now and always will, sometimes we have to take a few steps back to go forward. As a race we are always evolving and we always will. As I said this is how I see it all shifting and cleansing in the end.

Blessings.

Fiona Magpie Witch

My name is Fiona, I live in Rochdale with my two children and five cats. My true home is Somerset, it is where my heart will always be and I hope to return to my dear Avalon eventually. I am a practising Witch; I'm very eclectic in my work.

My totem is the magpie, her nature comes through me, enabling me to adapt and change any magical work to a way that suits me. I work very close with Nature and allow the various elements to guide me in my work. Of course the magpie features a lot in my practice and I listen to her subtle messages when she talks.
I am addicted to learning and absorb new knowledge daily. I live my life as a Witch working hand in hand with Nature and the Goddess; it is a part of my daily life and comes very naturally to me. I try to share a smile with everyone I meet and will always help anyone in need if I can.

I live my life with a positive outlook and will always be a friend to anyone who has an open mind an honest heart.

The Ancient Drum

At times it feels as though the path I walk is a solitary one, but that is not necessarily true. My course is a well-trodden route set by ancient ancestors and I am guided down it by primal energies. Voices from the past draw me to ancient ceremonies in chant and prayer that speak of song and celebration, preparing for the hunt, celebrating a birth or a life ended. And I hear the beating of the drum, pumping blood through my veins as the vitality of multitudes spin and entice me through centuries gone by.

My ancestral path guides me to the healers of villages, dreamers, scribes and poets like a grandmother leads the young through woods and forests to teach them the lore of plants, trees and herbs, passing on knowledge as valuable as gold and pointing to stars, the Sun and the Moon.

I experience ancient celebrations guided by the wheel of time: bounteous harvest festivals, epic fights between Holly and Oak, the subtle blending of light and dark, celebrations of birth and death and re-birth, from the beginning of time. Still the drum beats loud and clear.Standing in silent reflection on lives lost and paths followed, I recoil at the fierce heat of the flame that cut their journey short but admire their strength and fortitudes so much that pride rises in me and soothes the burn. Persecution and death made endurance so much stronger and the drum beats on, more footsteps on my journey.

I walk this path as a solitary, eclectic by choice, but millions of feet join me. Ancient minds guide me with knowledge that time cannot age and I follow their voices and music, I listen to their songs and poetry as I walk on and on. I am taught ancient lore, still precious and true and always, the drum, the heartbeat, the life force, beats on and on.

The Circle

I step in to the centre of the room. The only light is the gentle, golden glow of the scattered array of candles that dance upon the walls as I place four tea-light candles down to mark four points around me and set a symbolic object in front of each one. I light the first candle, embellished by a feather, and welcome the Eastern Guardian of Air as the flame flickers in to life. Turning clockwise to the next candle, which is adorned by a single copper coin, I light it and welcome the Southern Guardian of Fire before turning to the next candle, gilded with a shell to embody the Western Guardian of Water, whom I welcome with a light of the candle. Finally I turn to the fourth candle and before it lay a stone to represent the Northern guardian of earth. I give my final welcome as I light the Northern candle and then return to the centre, now encompassed in and protected by the elements.

Wand comfortably in my right hand and pointing east, I turn slowly deosil and as I do so, a white light forms a perfect circle around me, starting as a gentle shimmer that vivifies into a deep, shielding glow when the circle is closed. In the centre of the circle stand two more tea-lights, which I ignite one at a time, first welcoming the Goddess to my sacred space, who announces her presence with a tender glint of silver light, and then the God who arrives with a gentle flicker of gold. Raising my arms, I declare the circle closed.

It is now a sacred place of perfect love and perfect trust, with the raised energy creating a wall of pure white light; potently sheltering and exclusively pleasant. So I gradually lower my arms, close my eyes and simply stand, absorbing the energies dancing within my sacred space.

As I take in the energy, we become one; the circle and I so I sit down to be at one with my Lord and Lady. But the energy is so overwhelming; I stretch out my hand and fervently touch the shimmering wall of my sacred space. A warm glow travels through my fingers, along my arms and pulses through my body; I am rejuvenated and more alive than ever before. And my eyelids flutter shut despite myself as I fall in to still meditation, the blessed space now wholly a part of me and I a part of it because the Goddess and God have drawn closer, they speak to me and I to them; we three are one within this sacred circle. So I linger. The divine essence of safety and joy, rejuvenation and life envelopes me within the wall of unadulterated light and energy, and I am left in spiritual fulfillment. But after many blissful minutes, it is time to leave.

First I bid farewell and blessed be to my Lord and Lady, extinguishing their candles but never the light provide in my life. The Guardians of the elements too gain my blessing and farewell before I quench their flames, one by one and then rise to my feet.

With wand in hand once more, I stand again in the middle of my sacred space and turn slowly widdershins, returning to where I started and raising my arms to declare the circle open. A rush of magick dispels in to the Universe, enriching the very fabric of the earth and cleansing every particle of air.

Stepping outside, I slip off my shoes and stand barefoot in the garden, feeling the energy I raised becoming grounded and returned to the earth from where it was borrowed. And then I return to my room, the candle light gently flickering as I sit down and suddenly catch a gentle white shimmer of light on the floor; the circle has been opened, but never broken.

The Wish

Today a spell was cast with words unspoken,
The Universal spirits and elements were suddenly awoken
A silent wish uttered that nobody heard:
A whisper to the air, caught by a bird.
The bird passed it on to the leaves on the trees,
 And whispered to the Universe as they swayed in the breeze.
The decision was made, the answer was clear,
The birds in the wood sang loud in a cheer.
A single, loan figure stood barefoot in the grass,
Hands outstretched, she'd found the courage to finally ask.
Unbeknown to her, assent was already given,
The elemental guardians were now most ardently driven.
Privilege was given to the bird, the answer to deliver,
Her heart was full of melancholy, he would be the hope giver.
Hands outstretched, she was ready to speak, but suddenly came a delicate caress.
A single white feather, a resounding YES!

A Day in my Life

I open my eyes in the early hours of the morning and the first thing I do is offer earnest gratitude to my Lord and Lady for a restful night and a fresh day. Rising, I make my coffee and with cup in hand, I step out of my back door to the joy of my world and the very center of my being; my wood.

The dawn chorus is already melodically rejoicing the start of the brand new day. Magpies, finches, blackbirds, thrushes and crows, all full of gratitude and in harmony connected, sing their song for the Goddess. The trees bow and wave regally in the gentle breeze as if to say, "Good morning, welcome to today!" The early morning air is unpolluted and smells divinely crisp, expelling the old and stale air of yesterday. I fill my lungs with fresh air, thus beginning my day, as always, with contentment and joy.

As I go about my daily chores, I am mindful of how others travel their path, and to those who are quite sad and carrying a heavy burden, I share a smile and for a second I see them shine, shoulders loosening and faces lighting up in a flicker of emotion. I like to believe that such a simple gesture of compassion can help to make their spirit shift and give them the courage to endure. My time spent at home is filled with warmth, laughter and good conversation. We three are each other's support. We are happy and when one is down, we lift them up; it's what we've always done and always will do instinctively.

As the day recedes into night, I once again step outside to my oasis, my retreat, my escape and I'm welcomed by the dusk chorus, usually led by a single blackbird and a choir of crows. Their song winds me down and gives me time to reflect on how my day has been spent. As the blackbird sings I ask, 'how did I help my fellow man today? Did I make a difference? Was I able to reach out and make someone happy, even just for a little while?' As the blackbird finishes his song and flies to his nest, a calm silence falls. I stand hushed, grounded and humbled to be part of such a vast connection, like a web of fine strands that could affect any living thing with one gentle vibration.

Standing alone in my garden, I end my day the way I began it, with heartfelt thank you for my well spent day, grateful that I possibly caused happiness for someone, which, in turn, causes happiness for me. A bat flies over my head bringing me back to here and now. "In perfect love and perfect trust, my Lord and Lady!" I conclude, "Blessed Be!"

Laura Bos

Laura Bos is forever between places, at the moment home to her is the Worcestershire countryside. Laura loves the seasonal changes and is often to be found walking the hidden pathways and journeying across wild meadows. She paints and writes about the things she sees and feels upon these journeys, finding the magic in the smallest of things. She was blessed to have been brought up in rural Gloucestershire surrounded by an area rich in folklore and magic.

Her magical path is always unfolding, with the many twists and turns new insights are always forthcoming.

This green spirited soul lives with her husband Andy and together they enjoy a simple lifestyle of art and writing. In her spare time Laura has run workshops and has given talks on the simple ways we can honour the cycle of the seasons.

To contact Laura you are welcome to email her at the following address. Lore.feline@hotmail.co.uk

Journey

Daylight is beginning to yield and give way towards dusk, the day fades to a deep blue and the air stills in a moment of held bliss.

In a far off ash tree a tawny owl gives voice to the awakening night, testing his wings to take to flight. The energy shifts and stirs, hedgerows and field edges merge in the fading light, take on new forms and fill our minds with the voices of our ancestors.

The wind slowly stirs the blackthorn thicket, sharp spikes rub together releasing tales of winter and songs of frost. Stories of harsh and biting cold running deep within the land, spreading to every green and sheltered hollow.

High above the sky is dusted with the light of many stars, their pattern forming a be jeweled cloak to wrap around the milky white shoulders of the pale moon maiden as she looks down upon the land of the mother. Moving with light-footed grace over farm track pasture a fox is about her nightly hunt.

Her amber stare gazes upon lady moon for the briefest of moments, before the needs of her belly and that of her cubs stirs her mind back to its present quest.

Hedgerow banks are adrift with mugwort and dandelion cloaks, waving a spell of deep magic and whispered wisdom of ancient and yet awakening craft. All is seeding and growing with the ebb and flow of the sacred seasons. An ash key cast upon the night air settles upon the deep dark soil, soon to find a place within the mother to transform and change. Thus begins a journey from sleeping seed to future tree, blessed by the elements and honoured in the hearts of those yet to come.

A spider is weaving amongst the tall grasses, her web so fine, a trap of beauty . Spinner of fate in her own right, patience and crone like wisdom she spins in the elements of this sacred land. Songs of barley fields inter-spaced with swollen brown rivers at spring high tides, tales of sacred trees who's sap flows the colour of the mother's life blood, springs rising up from deep within the belly of the earth a place of offerings and invocations.

A moth settles for a moment upon the leaf of a red clover plant, its pale wings reflecting the soft and light of the moon high above. A creature of shadows and mystery, flying on silken wings courting the deep blue night.

A slight breeze stirs the grasses which line either side of the track made by creatures about their nightly business.

The moment seems to hang like spoken words, a ghostly song of the land, a breath from the past returning to its roots at the very heart of this sacred landscape. Land that has been shaped by the elements and weathered by the seasons. A place of our ancestors and those yet to be.

John Awen & Jhyenan O'Shea

Song of the earth

Let the song of the woods be heard
Of the many hue leaves cast upon the wind
To rest like dreams on this sacred ground
Let it flow like fast moving rivers at Equinox tide
Let it put down deep roots into the rich and nourishing earth
Let it rise with the first flowers to herald the light of spring returning
As the rain in April dances down upon the greening earth
Let it create trickles, ripples and blessings for the awakening land
Let all trees bud and reach higher for Zenith as he brings the lighter days
Give your voice to the oak, a mighty giant who holds the heart- beat of this place
He who remembers all forests past
Whisper words of comfort to the healing springs

Watery womb of our mother and healer spirit
Tie ribbons on Clootie trees to dance and spin in the wind
Tie one for this beautiful earth, one for a dear friend and one for your hopes
Embrace the night on a starry eve and honour Lady moon
Draw and drink of her essence, her many faces, her visions and her stories
Find that inner wild woman and let her loose
Let her roar with passion and power of this surging earth
Wild, untamed and burning
Whisper words of sweetness under hawthorn bough
Honey eyed and sugar blessing, humming the return of summer in golden evenings song
As the golden wheat ripens and sways in gentle breeze
Dance and sing in honour of the harvest
Fashion corn maidens under the shinning harvest moon
Leave one at meadows edge in blessing the abundance of Mother Earth
Drum earths deep heart beat by standing stone
Join your voice to the ancient song

Connect with those who have woven the tales and stories of the land
Share the same breath, give voice to the echo
Let the magic stir your heart
May you dance lightly upon the Mother
May the sun give you hope
May the moon guide you dreams
May you honour this place, to pass on to the others that come after you.

The Turning

Sun bathes amber fields in saffron hues, as summers day draws towards evening. The machines of harvest stand watching, cooling as the heat of day wanes once more to the night and stillness.

Gentle breeze stirs the leaves of the oak lord, watcher at the dawn light, sovereign to the land. He has stood here and seen the land be toiled and worked, shaped by the hands of man, carved by beast and machine.

He has seen the soil bring forth abundance and riches from the bounty of the earth mother. Green gives way to rusty gold and natures dance uptakes.

The palest of crescents glides into view singing the sweetest of songs, lamenting the journey towards summers end. In the stillness of evening, a chill is felt giving flesh to autumn's bones, a form returning to cast jewels on every hedgerow and bring mist to the darkening of the days.

Wisdom shall drip from the elder tree crone, her berries rich in darkness and magic.

Hawthorn shall cloak herself in crimson red amongst the turning leaves.

The veil shall once again thin, lace like and full of mystery and secrets.

The shades of the past shall once again walk the old paths unchanged, a memory, a folklore returning to this sacred and woven landscape.

But for now it is still a place of golden fields and high hopes, of harvest and dreams. Spirit of summer rises, takes her place on the floor and dances the cycle of the seasons.

As the richness of the poppy, the deep blue of the corn flower begin to fade upon this her earthy gown, she lifts her head to the pale beauty of the moon maiden.

Summer closes her eyes and a smile crosses her serine face, she knows that the time is drawing near when the earth shall call her into her embrace and together they shall journey to the place of rest and sleep.

Times change and seasons flow, rise and fall, for it is the way of all things. From sky to earth, from growth to sleep, all as it has always been. But in truth, with every ending there is always a beginning.

Painting by Laura Bos

This concludes our book, we hoped you have enjoyed reading it.
We send you our Brightest Blessings.

Jhyenan O'Shea and John Awen can be contacted at
spiritofawen@yahoo.com.

Made in the USA
Charleston, SC
07 January 2015